I0172645

Driftwood at the River's Edge
and other cutup poems

by Peter Wortsman

BAMBOO
DART
PRESS

LOS ANGELES † NEW YORK † LONDON † MELBOURNE

Driftwood at the River's Edge by Peter Wortsman

978-1-947240-89-6   Paperback

978-1-947240-90-2   eBook

Cover art by Harold Wortsman

Cover photograph by Seth Rothstein

Layout and design by Peter Wortsman and Mark Givens

For information:

Bamboo Dart Press

chapbooks@bamboodartpress.com

Bamboo Dart Press 042

Pelekinesis
www.pelekinesis.com

BAMBOO DART PRESS
www.bamboodartpress.com

SHRiMPER
www.shrimperrecords.com

"Shadow boxes become poetic theater or settings wherein are metamorphosed the elements of a childhood pastime. The fragile, shimmering globules become the shimmering but more enduring planets — a connotation of moon and tides — the association of water less subtle, as when driftwood pieces make up a proscenium to set off the dazzling white of sea foam and billowy cloud crystallized in a pipe of fancy."

Joseph Cornell

Contents

Lost and Found
(a foreword)

I recently lost a bag containing, among other objects of no
pecuniary value but of considerable personal import, my
address book, an agenda with upcoming appointments and
events penciled in, and a notebook of freshly cut cutup poems
flattened and preserved like butterflies and wild flowers. First I
cursed, then I cried, then I tried to console myself with the
thought that most of the names in the address book belonged
to people I could no longer even associate with a face; as to the
vanished agenda, doctors' offices generally call to remind of
upcoming appointments; and the words of the rearranged
cutup poems in the lost notebook didn't belong to me to begin
with. I rationalized the loss. Do we not lose things for a reason?
Have they not perhaps outlived their usefulness, weigh us
down, and need to be dropped like ballast from a hot air
balloon to lighten the load? Then I remembered that I had
previously scanned the texts as an electronic record to post on
social media. Some of the scans were badly done. But the
originals are in any case gone for good, and these facsimiles,
faulty though they may be, a bit like memory itself, and like
the pencil rubbings of old tombstones twice removed from the
disintegrating self, preserve a telling footprint. No choice but to

accept the loss as a literary constraint and generative factor in the process of composition, along with razor blade, scissors and glue, to winnow out the fibrous husk and preserve only the germ of meaning. As I did with Borrowed Words, my previous collection of cutups, I juxtapose a copy of the untidy original text with a tightened transcript to give the reader a taste of the process.

Peter Wortsman
October 12, 2022

driftwood at the river's edge

collecting the rubbish

artifacts.
    fierce things,

things that seemed
    beyond me

raw and timeless

still lifes, land-

scapes --

let the

stuff

be

itself,

give it room to breathe

enjoy-

ing it for exactly what it

is

there's something happening that we can't
control.

Driftwood at the River's Edge

Collecting the rubbish:
artifacts,
fierce things,
things that seemed
beyond me,
raw and timeless
still-lifes, land-
scapes –
let the
stuff
be
itself,
give it room to breathe –
enjoy-
ing it for exactly what it
is;
there's something happening that we can't
control.

What is a poem?

this feeling of infinity

from a shopping list to Shakespeare.

these words,

the inside out,
like you're wearing someone else's clothes.

(Lacking pa-
per, he tested his hypotheses by writing on
a teacup with a stolen pen.)

TO FIND A FORM that accommodates the mess

AUGUST 28, 2022

What is a Poem?

This feeling of infinity
from a shopping list to Shakespeare,
these words,
the inside out,
like you're wearing someone else's clothes.
Lacking pa-
per, he tested his hypotheses by writing on
a teacup with a stolen pen,
to find a form that accommodates the mess.

August 28, 2022

a poem

a new kind of Chinese typewriter.

a fishing net, it stretches to hold more than
initially seemed possible.

vastness,
the coiled interior

a silent assembly of

words

MARCH 4, 2022

A Poem

A new kind of Chinese typewriter;
a fishing net, it stretches to hold more than
initially seemed possible:
vastness,
the coiled interior,
a silent assembly of
words.

March 4, 2022

the mind of
        thought

among the world's intangible
    practices.

    thought

    hints of things, synaptic touches
    that trigger

    trillions of tiny

    larval

      idea

       nets

      often festooned with flamboyant,
streaming appendages

    ideas

    so delicate \
mushed into a gelatinous goo

    "We've been doing this for
years, but it's still new,"

APRIL 13, 2021

The Mind of
Thought

Among the world's intangible
    practices,
    thought
    hints of things, synaptic touches
    that trigger
        trillions of tiny
           larval
               idea
                    nets,
           often festooned with flamboyant,
       streaming appendages,
            ideas
            so delicate,
       mushed into a gelatinous goo.
           "We've been doing this for
           years, but it's still new."

April 13, 2021

the good things in life.

I've spent my life

collecting

a landfill of

inky

unscripted

useless things

dirt

beneath my fingernails and

all the inexact,

flawed

moments

of

confusion,

fear,

and

doubt

MARCH 4, 2022

The Good Things in Life

I've spent my life
collecting
a landfill of
inky,
unscripted,
useless things,
dirt
beneath my finger nails and
all the inexact,
flawed
moments
of
confusion,
fear,
and
doubt.

March 4, 2022

the mystery of things

take something ordinary
and find beauty in it.

a talisman.

accidentally
timeless

exquisite, de-
natured and almost entirely contentless.

I took to it. I like its simplicity,

"It's one thing to look at .
another thing to hold

'It's so tactile,

I regularly kiss   it,'

different
beautiful

the simple pleasures of
sinuous line

it occupies space and a moment in

time.

APRIL 13, 2021

The Mystery of Things

Take something ordinary
and find beauty in it,
a talisman,
accidentally
timeless,
exquisite de-
natured and almost entirely contentless.
I took to it. I like its simplicity.
It's one thing to look at,
another thing to hold.
It's so tactile,
I regularly kiss it.
Different,
beautiful,
the simple pleasures of
sinuous line,
it occupies space and a moment in
time.

April 13, 2021

NATURE MORTE

mind
sense
thing

like mirrors and
the root .

like waves of the sea

like
this wilted plant that finally got the water

MAY 9, 2021

Nature Morte

Mind,
sense,
thing,

like mirrors and
the root,
like waves of the sea,

like
this wilted plant that finally got the water.

May 9, 2021

Date

landscape
surgery

soundlessly, wordlessly

scribbled across the

the wilds

(a leaf doesn't
need language to communicate),

in Druidic thinking,

trees were viewed
as sentient beings that connected the Earth
to the heavens.

MARCH 20, 2022

Landscape
Surgery

Soundlessly, wordlessly,
scribbled across
the wilds
(a leaf doesn't
need language to communicate);
in Druidic thinking
trees were viewed
as sentient beings that connected the Earth
to the heavens.

March 20, 2022

illegible piece of skywriting.

the punctuation gets notice-
ably idiosyncratic.

The bizarre markings,

collagelike

limitless.

arcs and spirals

dashes and squiggles
graphed.

each scurrying dot

a

vessel

of

"vast nothingness"

SEPTEMBER 4, 2022

Illegible Piece of Skywriting

The punctuation gets notice-

ably idiosyncratic:

the bizarre markings,

collagelike,

limitless

arcs and spirals

graphed,

each scurrying dot

a

vessel

of

vast nothingness.

September 4, 2022

Magic Eye.

looking at
things

the way a racehorse leaves the
starting gate.

I

project myself into their bodies

somebody else's reality is.

my

infinity mirror

a canvas upon which .

The layers of inquiry are endless,

"I want it all, now"

MARCH 28, 2021

Magic Eye

Looking at
things
the way a racehorse leaves the
starting gate,

I
project myself into their bodies;
somebody else's reality is
my
infinity mirror,
a canvas upon which
the layers of inquiry are endless.
I want it all now.

March 28, 2021

Virtual reality

I could see out the window in the back,

in the secret, decaying spaces

amid the refuse.

different versions of the same

present tense, stitched together from a patchwork of memories —

We're always competing against ghosts of the past

It is as if I am reliving another person's

life,

not my own.

SEPTEMBER 11, 2022

Virtual Reality

I could see out the window in the back,
in the secret, decaying spaces
amid the refuse,
different versions of the same
present tense stitched together from a
patchwork of memories –
we're always competing against
ghosts of the past.
It is as if I am reliving another person's
life,
not my own.

September 11, 2022

the naked, banal reality of this
thing that will come to us all."

We all age. We all lose things.

The details matter.

endless variations

of

the quivering Jell-O

of

life

"You try to predict, but in the end you
get surprises."

My crystal ball is broken,

it's possible that we will never be-
come perfect prophets

SEPTEMBER 11, 2022

The Naked, Banal Reality of This Thing That Will Come to Us All

We all age. We all lose things.

The details matter:

endless variations

of

the quivering Jell-O

of

life.

You try to predict, but in the end you

get surprises.

My crystal ball is broken.

It's possible that we will never be-

come perfect prophets.

September 11, 2022

talking genitalia

intimacy comes through
a catalog

I love collecting

bodily sounds,

the

physicality of
time

'Sperm is a drop

of

delirium

Left behind

APRIL 7, 2022

Talking Genitalia

Intimacy comes through
a catalogue.
I love collecting
bodily sounds,
the
physicality of
time.
Sperm is a drop
of
delirium
left behind.

April 7, 2022

HOW WE FEEL about time

Very few people have plans for

The infinite

tethered, to

the knotty

Now.

They don't seem concerned

with

The question of becoming,

The flashes of
come and go

the weight of time."

Can you imagine a man,'
"too busy to go to his

funeral ?

APRIL 6, 2022

How We Feel About Time

Very few people have plans for
    the infinite,
    tethered to
        the knotty
        now,
        they don't seem concerned
        with
        the question of becoming,
    the flashes of
    come and go,
                the weight of time.

                Can you imagine a man
                too busy to go to his

                    funeral?

April 6, 2022

time will tell

time
crushed

raw

instinct

into words

; MARCH 22, 2022

Time Will Tell

Time
crushed
raw
instinct
into words.

March 22, 2022

a remedy for insomnia

try something new,

create a new language

a legacy

of

caustic
loss,

interrogate
cliché.

listen to
time

The curious,

uncertainty.

closing in

Like a fired bullet

FEBRUARY 21, 2022

A Remedy for Insomnia

Try something new:
    create a new language,
       a legacy
          of
              caustic
              loss;
       interrogate
       cliché,
             listen to
             time,
                   the curious
                         uncertainty,
                            closing in
                              like a fired bullet.

February 21 2022

"Self-Portrait."

a memory
a place
a person

as a mouth
as a metaphor

I still don't
know exactly what form it will take.

I re-

call the collective quiver and shrinking

a siren cry
and chutzpah

and

the silences that
define

this weird in-between place,

somewhere between
a premonition and déjà vu,

remain in the "now."

MARCH 30, 2021

Self Portrait

A memory,
a place,
a person
as a mouth,
as a metaphor.

I still don't
know exactly what form it will take.
I re-
call the collective quiver and shrinking,
a siren cry
and chutzpah
and
the silences that
define
this weird in-between place,
somewhere between
a premonition and déjà vu,
remain in the now.

March 30, 2021

sonic deluge

words seemed to echo

the hushed silence

The mesh beneath me vibrated and shook with sound waves, like a spider in its web.

, like courtiers
around a king

"It's how he heard things,"

how a humble
ballpoint pen became a microphone, a stage, a shield or a sword.

SEPTEMBER 2, 2022

Sonic Deluge

Words seemed to echo
the hushed silence;
the mesh beneath me vibrated and
shook with sound waves,
like a spider in its web,
like courtiers
around a king;
it's how we heard things,
how a humble
ballpoint pen became a microphone, a
stage, a shield, or a sword.

September 2, 2022

Art
cannot do everything.

the acoustics of

brain waves

mingling
assemblages,

with the

stroke of a pen,

fantasy, trapping the real
within it.

There has to be something left to
the imagination.

MAY 16, 2021

Art
Cannot Do Everything

The acoustics of

brain waves,

mingling

assemblages

with the

stroke of a pen,

fantasy trapping the real

within it.

There has to be something left to

the imagination.

May 16, 2021

mining for meaning,

. I'm a vessel of change.

a tapestry of

contradictory   desires,

boredom, curiosity, frustration.

catastrophe
freighted with

forlorn loneliness .
              and then some

others
      ...; rethink defi-

nitions

I keep thinking I'm going to grow u

Mining for Meaning

I'm a vessel of change,
a tapestry of
contradictory desires:
boredom, curiosity, frustration,
catastrophe
freighted with

forlorn loneliness,
and then some;
others
rethink defi-
nitions,

I keep thinking I'm going to grow up.

hypnotic
monologue

And so here we are.

The world is upside down

the barrier
has evaporated,

lucid dreaming has be-
come a kind of sport

It's quite a high-wire act,

sounding somewhere

in a stairwell

echoes

knocking on

My

dreams

JUNE 9 , 2021

Hypnotic Monologue

And so here we are.
The world is upside-down,
the barrier
has evaporated;
lucid dreaming has be-
come a kind of sport;
it's a high-wire act
sounding somewhere
in a stairwell,
echoes
knocking on
my
dreams.

June 9. 2021

in his oracular mode

most
desire
oblivion

forget
flesh

I

choose
ooze
recall

JUNE 9 , 2021

In His Oracular Mode

Most
desire
oblivion,

forget
flesh;

I

choose
ooze
recall.

June 9, 2021

Literati

He was this crazy hybrid

spontaneity, gravitas and other qualities

gone rogue

accused of soaking up "la cul-
ture américaine."

With

haute-street

fairy-tale fantasy

— a winking embrace of kitsch,

the perfect machine to
capture the fundamental fuzzi-
ness

In another life I would have written

an

unduly challenging
book

"I felt the need to turn over a new leaf," he
explained.

"No one takes a U-Haul to the cemetery,"

MARCH 11, 2021

Literati

He was this crazy hybrid:
spontaneity, gravitas and other qualities
gone rogue,
accused of soaking up "la cul-
ture américaine,"
with
haute-street
fairy tale fantasy
—a winking embrace of kitsch,
the perfect machine to
capture the fundamental fuzzi-
ness.
In another life I would have written
an
unduly challenging
book.
"I felt the need to turn over a new leaf," he
explained.
"No one takes a U-Haul to the cemetery."

March 11, 2021

"the weight of

the word."

masked and distanced.

lip syncing ..

intimacy

"There are two people in you at all times.

nerve,
climbed in next .

to direct
the impassive eye

In other words,

time to go
wild, and I did

with every syllable

"Every single w/ord

formed
face up
through
tough

fragility

the
toughness

touched ● every fiber

with forger's ink still dripping from his
finger.

APRIL 15, 2021

The Weight of
the Word

Masked and distanced,
lip syncing
intimacy,
there are two people in you at all times.
Nerve
climbed in next
to direct
the impassive eye,
in other words,
time to go
wild, and I did
with every syllable,
every single word
formed
face-up
through
tough
fragility,
the
toughness
touched every fiber
with forger's ink still dripping from his
finger.

April 15, 2021

Skin.

that fits you like you were born in it.

Easy care & easy wear.

molded cups and derrière.

So essential, no body should be without it.

**on
top of it all. Slip into**

Skin.

P.W.

Skin

Skin
that fits you like you were born in it,

easy care & easy wear,
molded cups and derrière,

so essential nobody should be without it,

on
top of it all, slip into
skin.

Acknowledgments

"Words Feel Insufficient Here" and "Advice for an Insomniac" were first published in the online journal *Unlost*. "A Poem," "How We Feel About Time," "A Remedy for Insomnia" and "Time Will Tell" originally appeared on the website *Love in the Time of Covid: A Chronicle of a Pandemic*. Thanks again to Mark Givens and Dennis Callaci, who helped shepherd these strange assemblages into print.

BAMBOO
DART
PRESS

112 N. Harvard Ave. #65
Claremont, CA 91711

chapbooks@bamboodartpress.com
www.bamboodartpress.com

www.ingramcontent.com/pod-product-compliance
Lightning Source LLC
Chambersburg PA
CBHW081643040426
42449CB00015B/3444